BOLD KIDS

MW01675333

Microbes

AMAZING AND INTRIGUING FACTS
CHILDREN'S SCIENCE BOOK

Microbes are microscopic creatures that live on Earth. They can be single-celled organisms or colonies of cells.

Despite their microscopic size, microbes can have very important effects on the environment. You can learn more about the different types of microbes in this book.

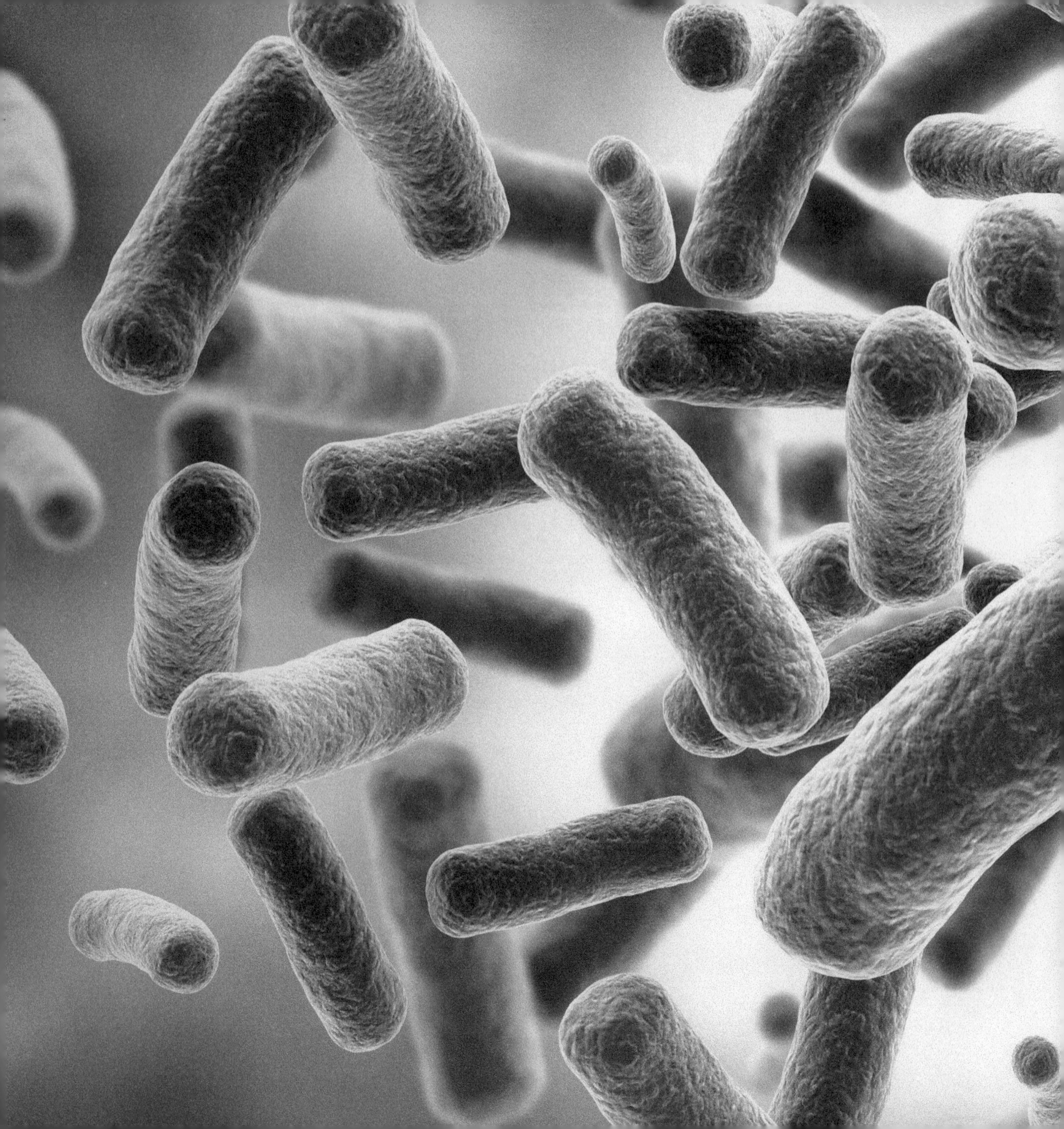

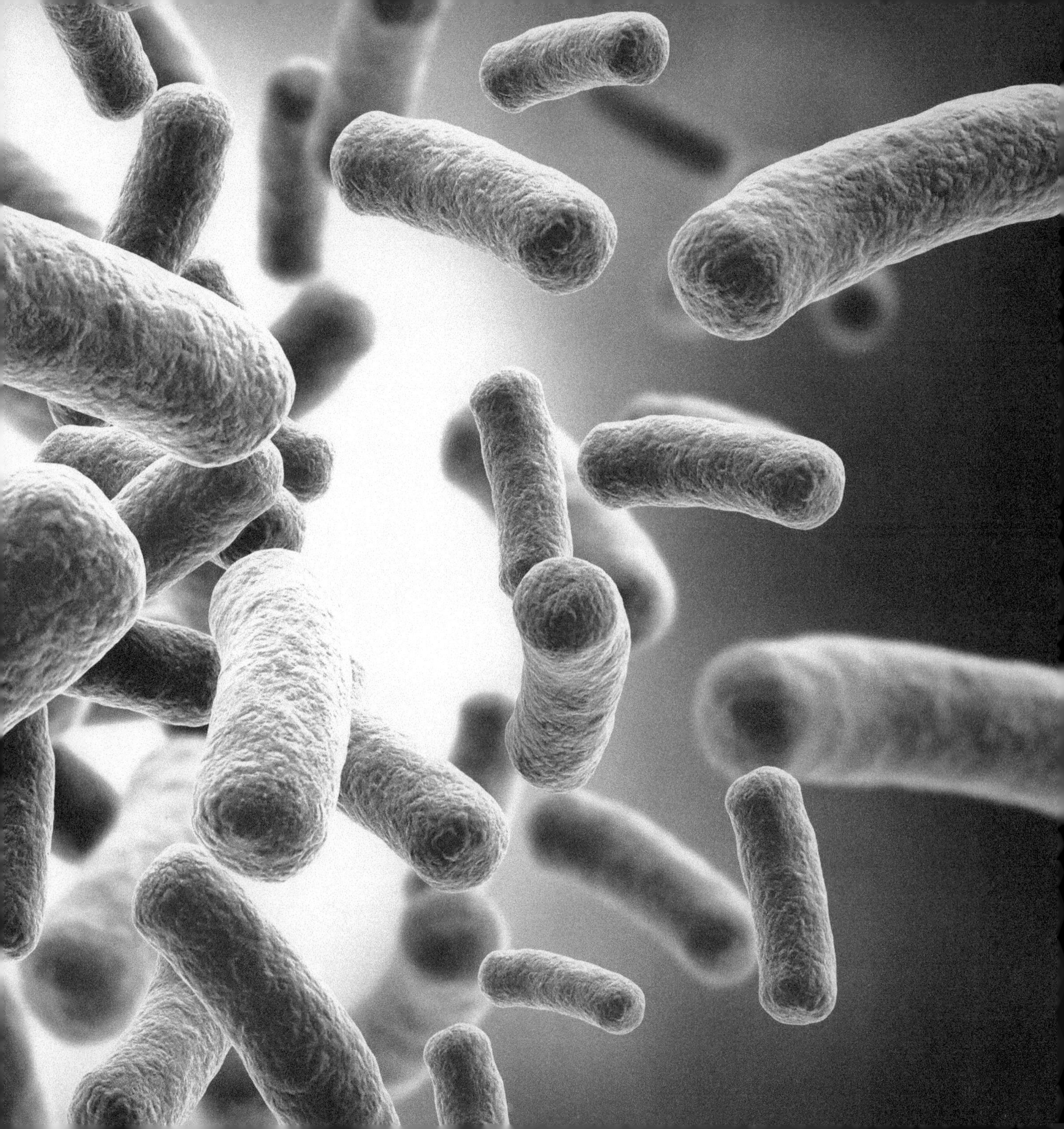

BACTERIA

Bacteria are multicellular, metabolically active organisms that divide by binary fission. They are one of the leading causes of disease and are common in our environment.

Although they appear to be simple forms of life, bacteria are highly complex and can use a wide range of hydrocarbon substrates for food, energy, and other essential processes. They are widely distributed and can adapt to their environments through evolution and selection of spontaneous mutations.

ARCHAEA

Archaea are members of the kingdom Archaea. Their evolution can be traced back to the last common ancestor of all living cells.

Archaea are souped-up bacteria, and their cell division process differs from that of eukaryotes. Scientists are still studying the internal workings of archaea. However, these organisms provide important clues for understanding the evolution of the nucleus and the division of cells.

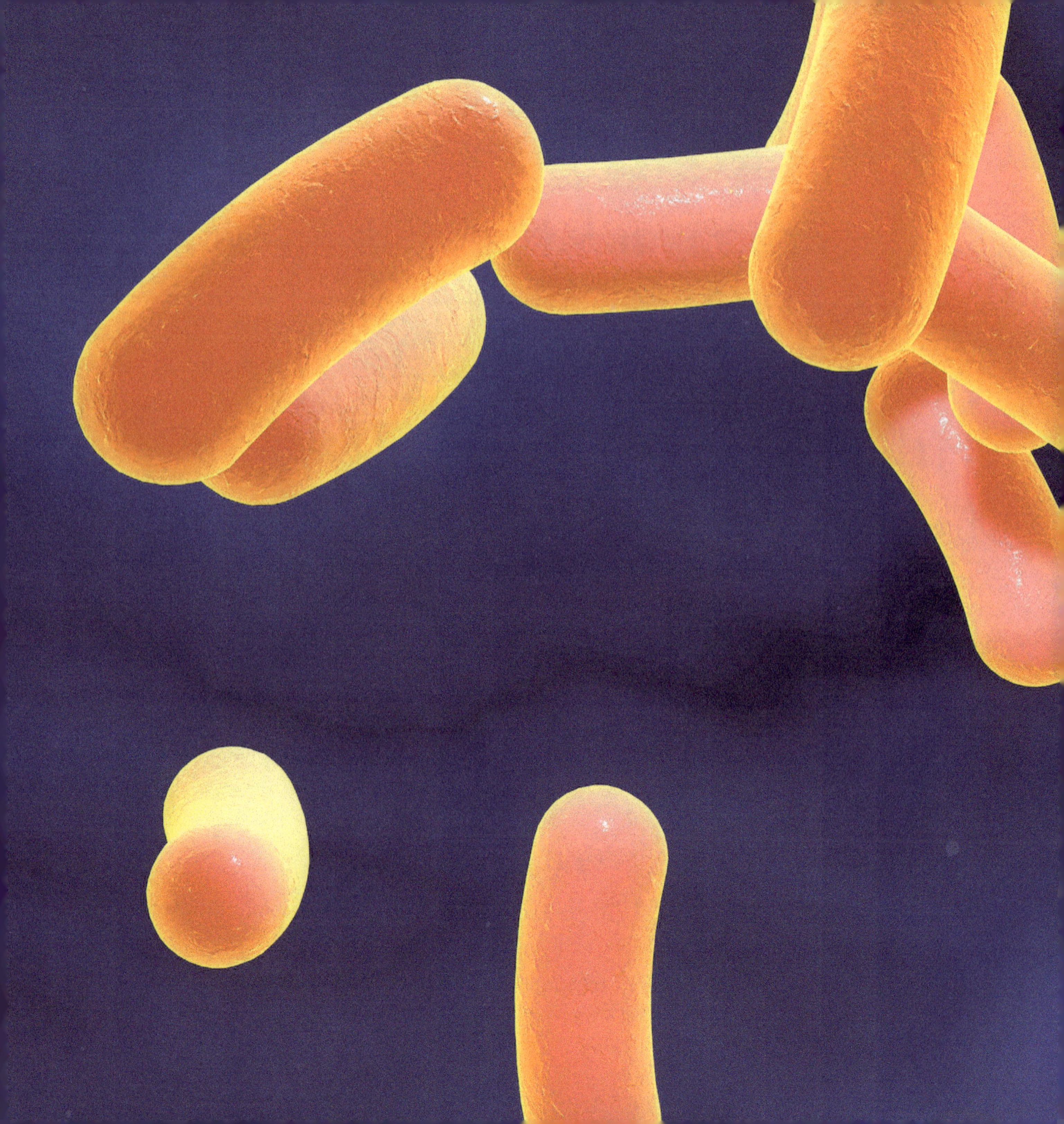

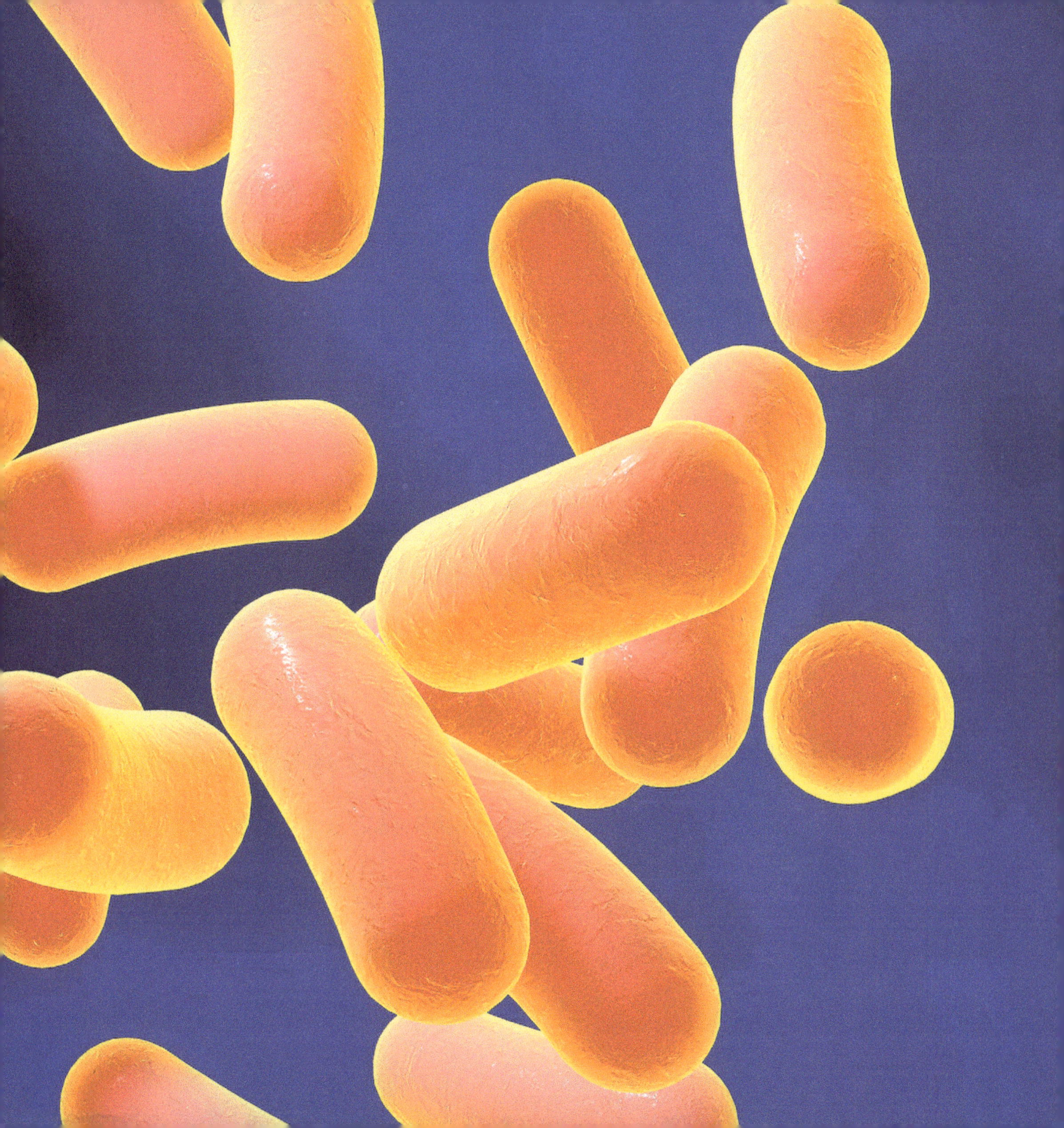

EUKARYOTA

The Eukaryota are a class of microbes. They have large cells with recognisable nuclei and nuclear membranes and internal filaments.

Some bacteria have similar structures but do not have filaments. Eukaryotes have several compartments that are useful for their various functions.

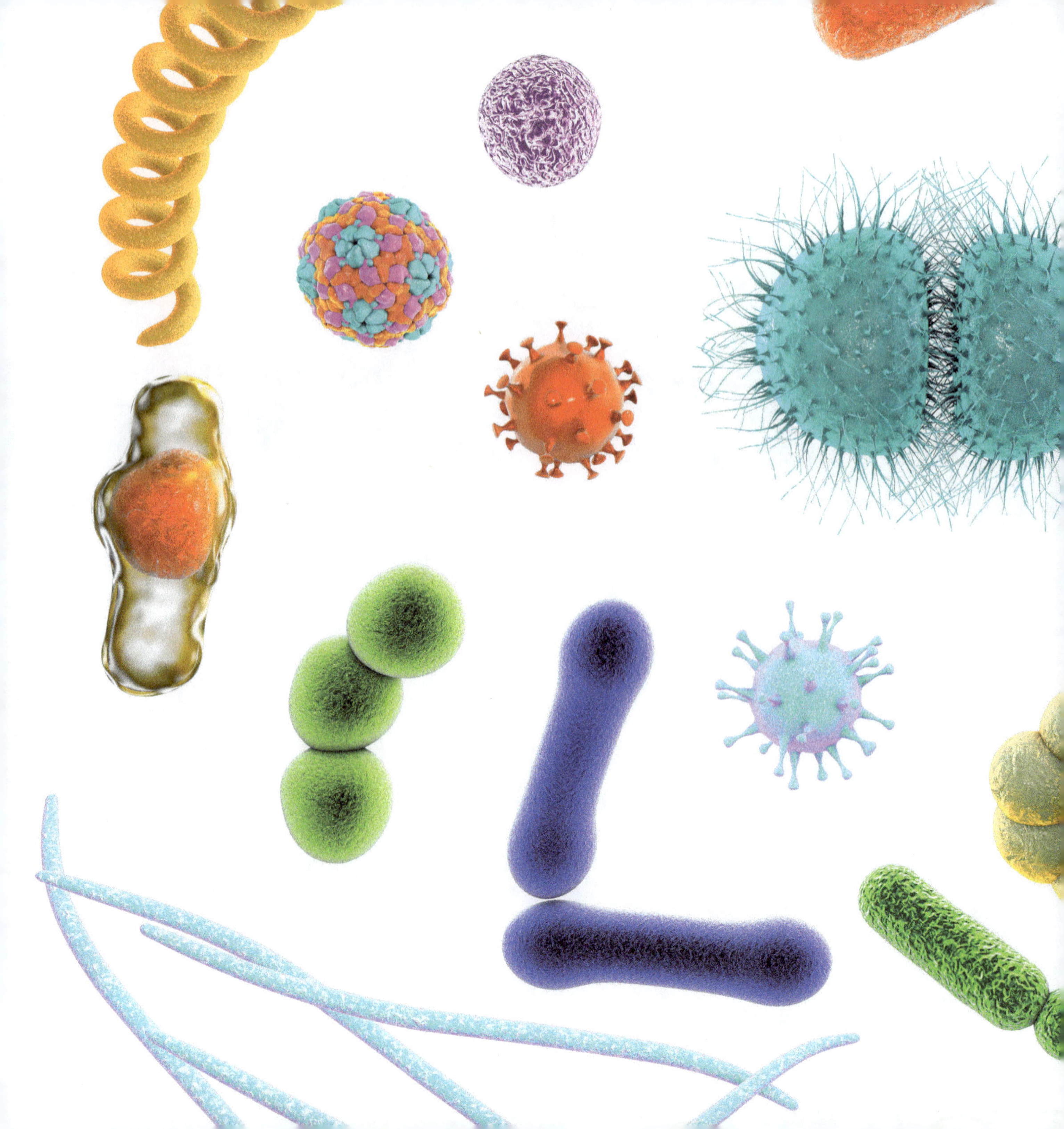

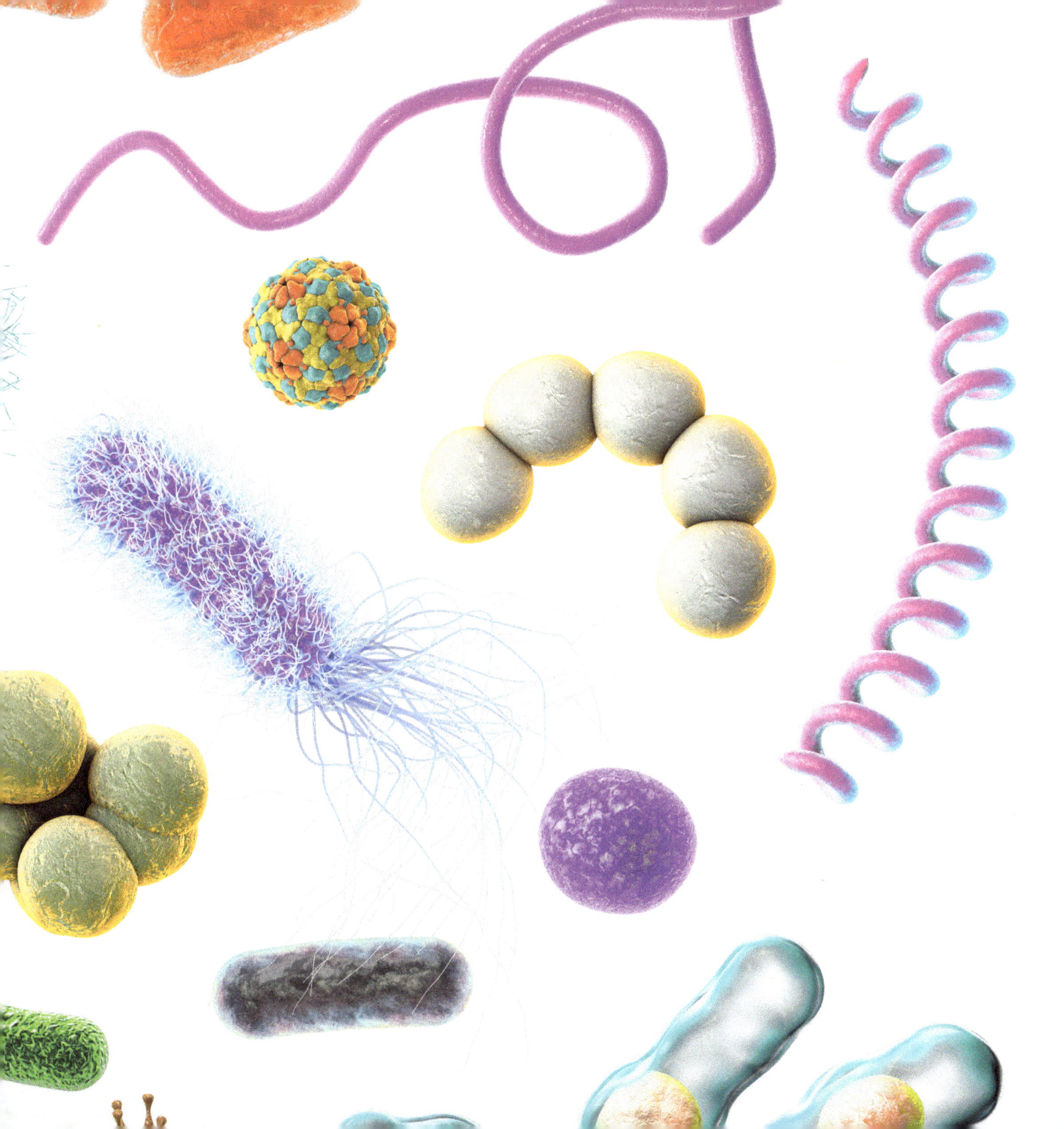

VIRUSES

Viruses are microscopic infectious agents that replicate within the living cells of their host. They cause disease and have been responsible for many epidemics throughout history.

Examples include the 2014 Ebola outbreak in West Africa and the 2009 swine flu pandemic. Viruses have also served as a powerful research tool, leading to new understanding of the mechanisms of protein synthesis and cellular processes.

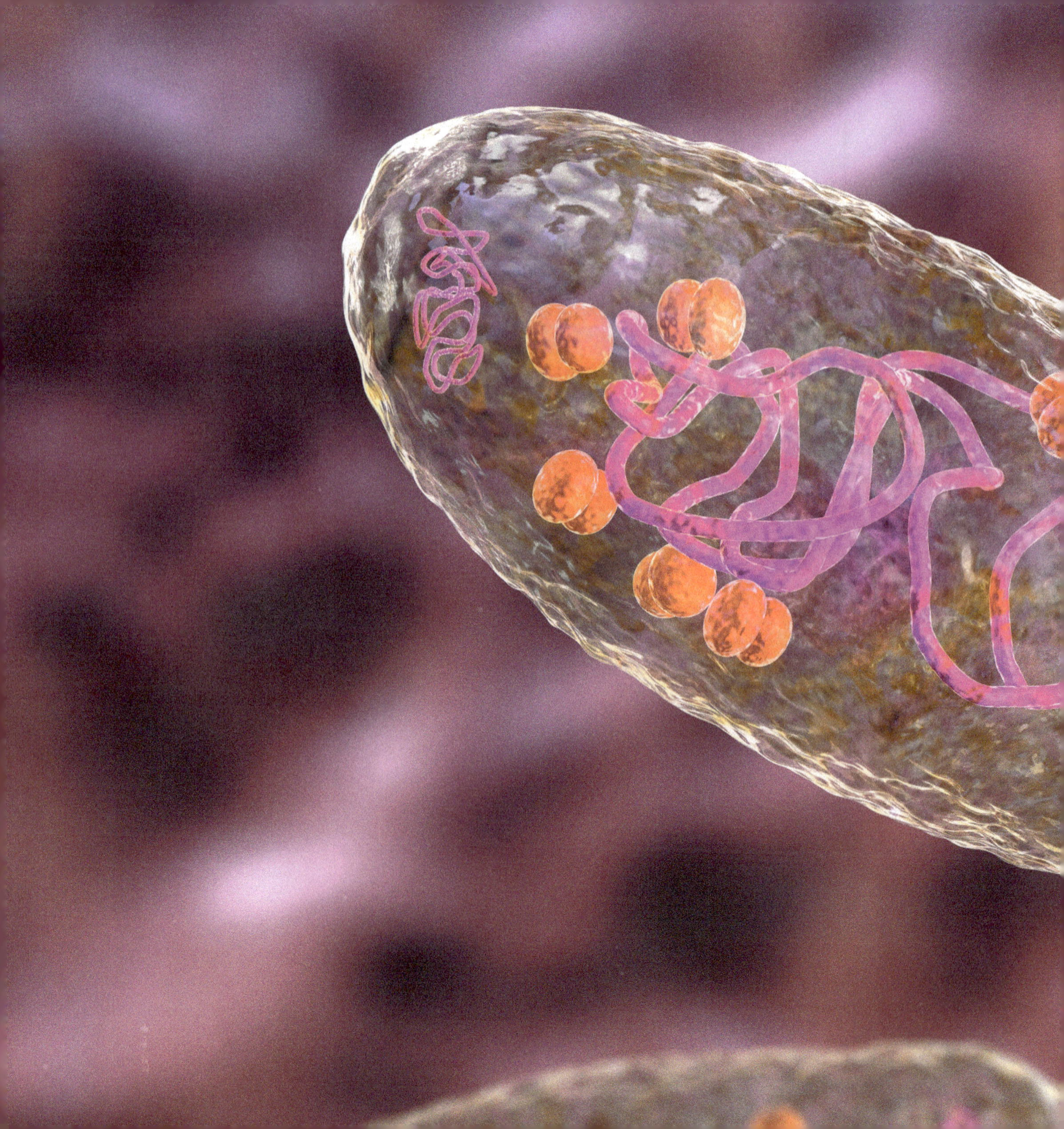

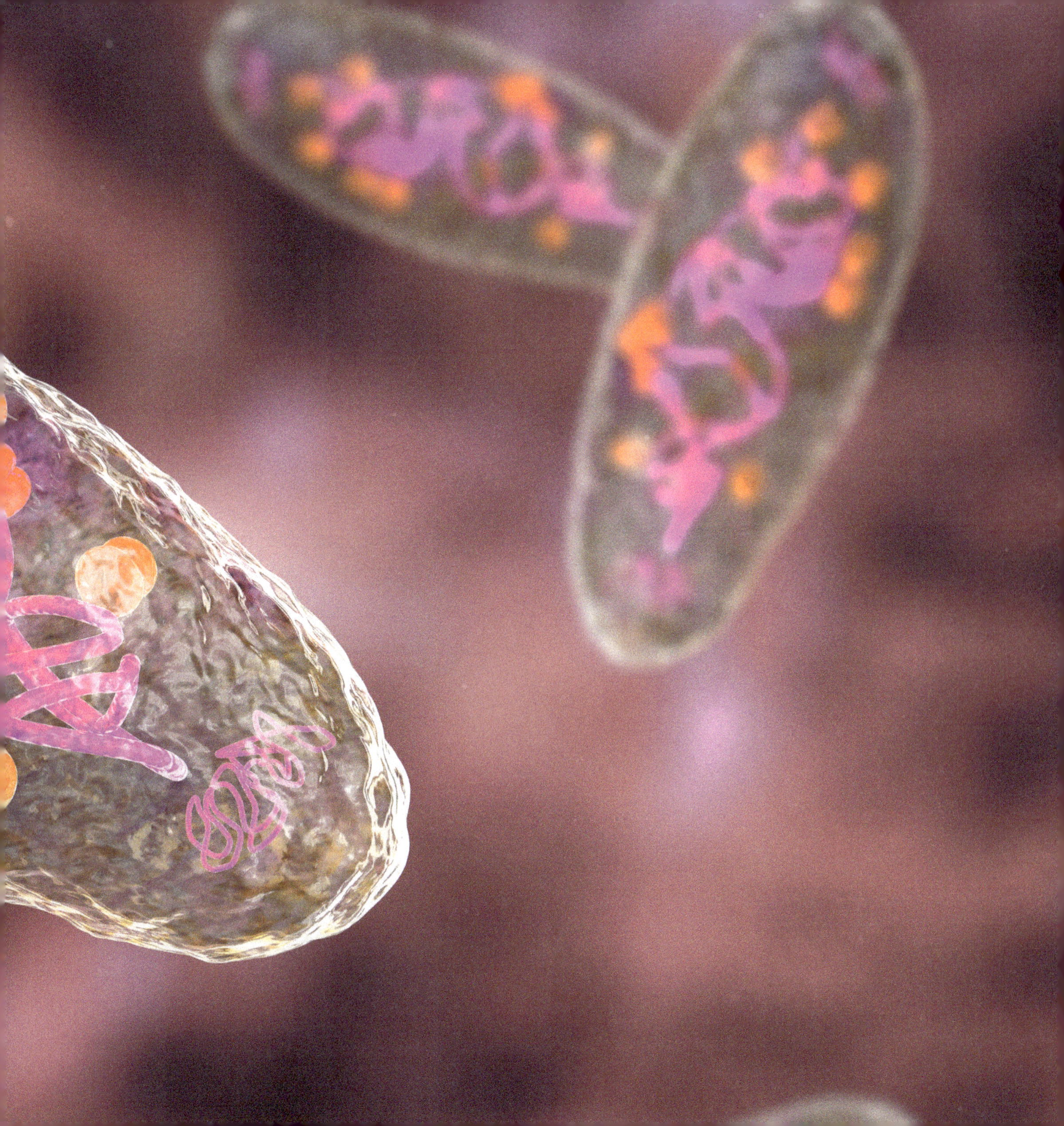

SYMBIOTA

Mammalian intestines are rich in indigenous bacterial communities, and most establish beneficial symbiotic relationships with their hosts.

This close proximity raises the question of why these bacteria may benefit their host, and how this symbiosis contributes to a host's overall health. In this article, we explore the role of immune suppression, subversion, and evasion in the development of symbiotic relationships.

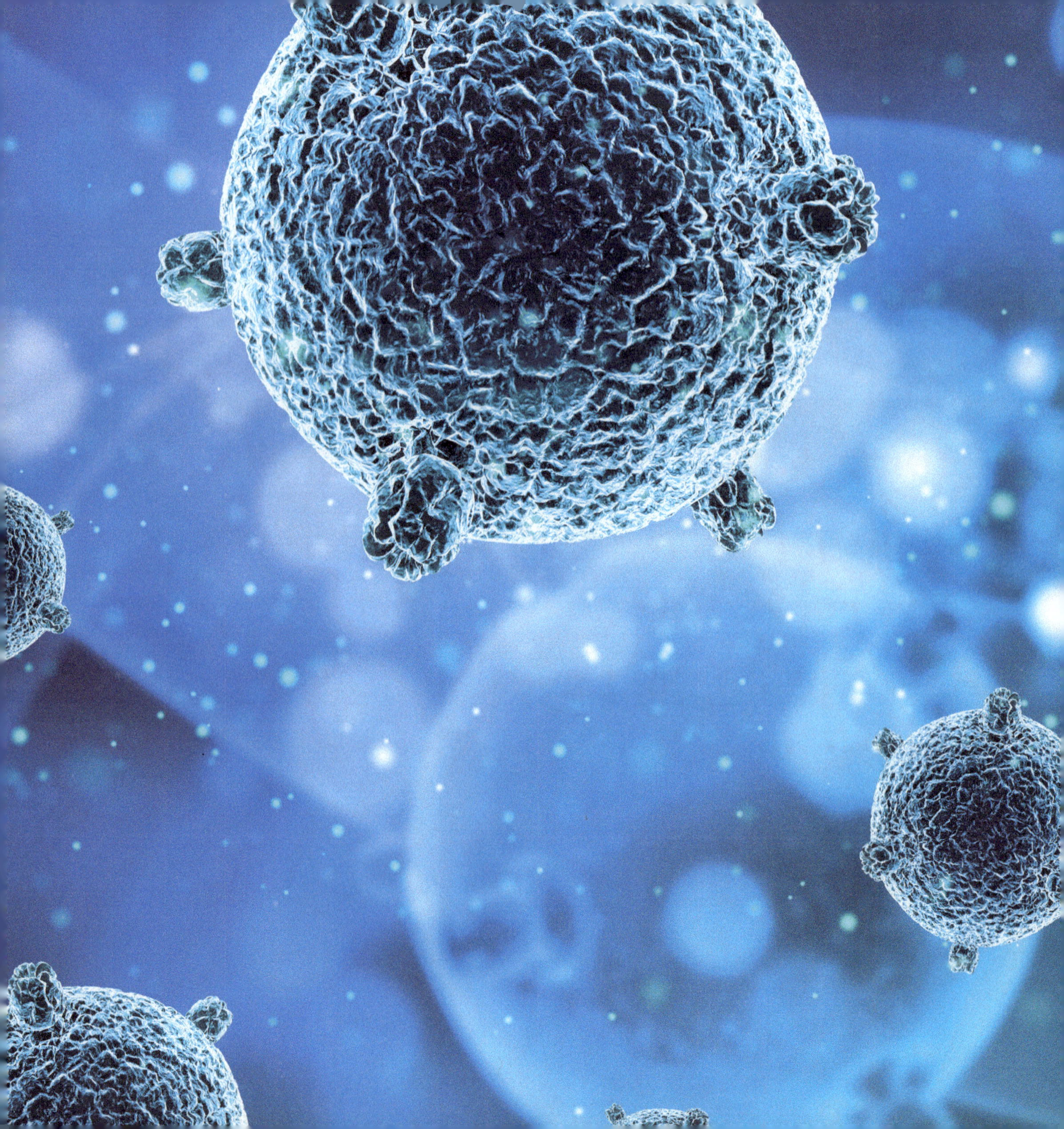

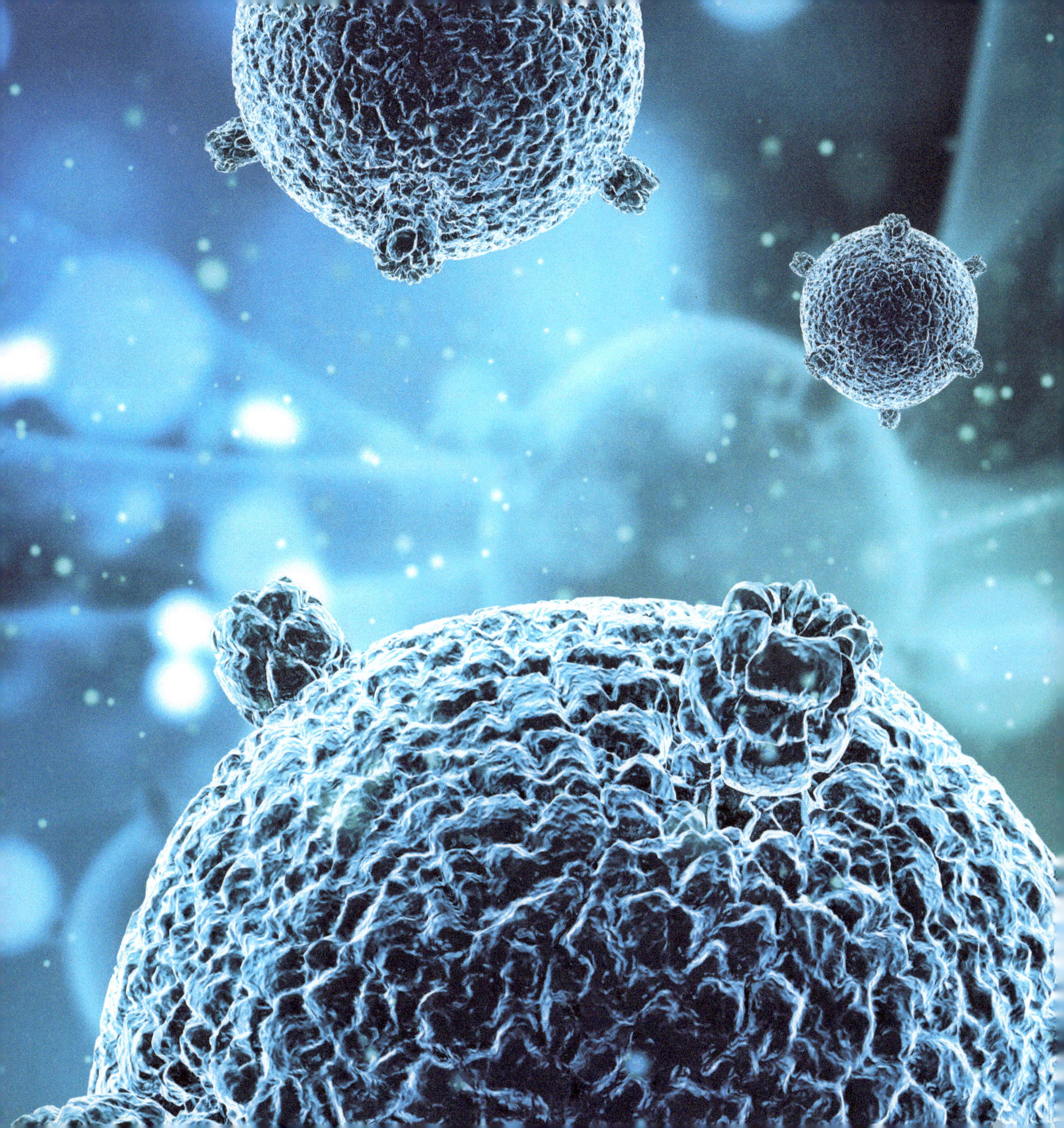

PARASITES

Microbes often develop parasites, allowing them to survive in new environments, forge novel associations, or even spread as a symbiosis with another organism.

Parasites can have a number of different traits that help them to survive in new environments, such as increased fitness, but they can also have selfish traits that can benefit their host.

ECTOPARASITES

Ectoparasites are small organisms that live on the surfaces of living things.

They are known as vectors of infectious disease, and some are even harmful to humans. Examples of ectoparasites include ticks, which transmit diseases to humans through the bite of their host.

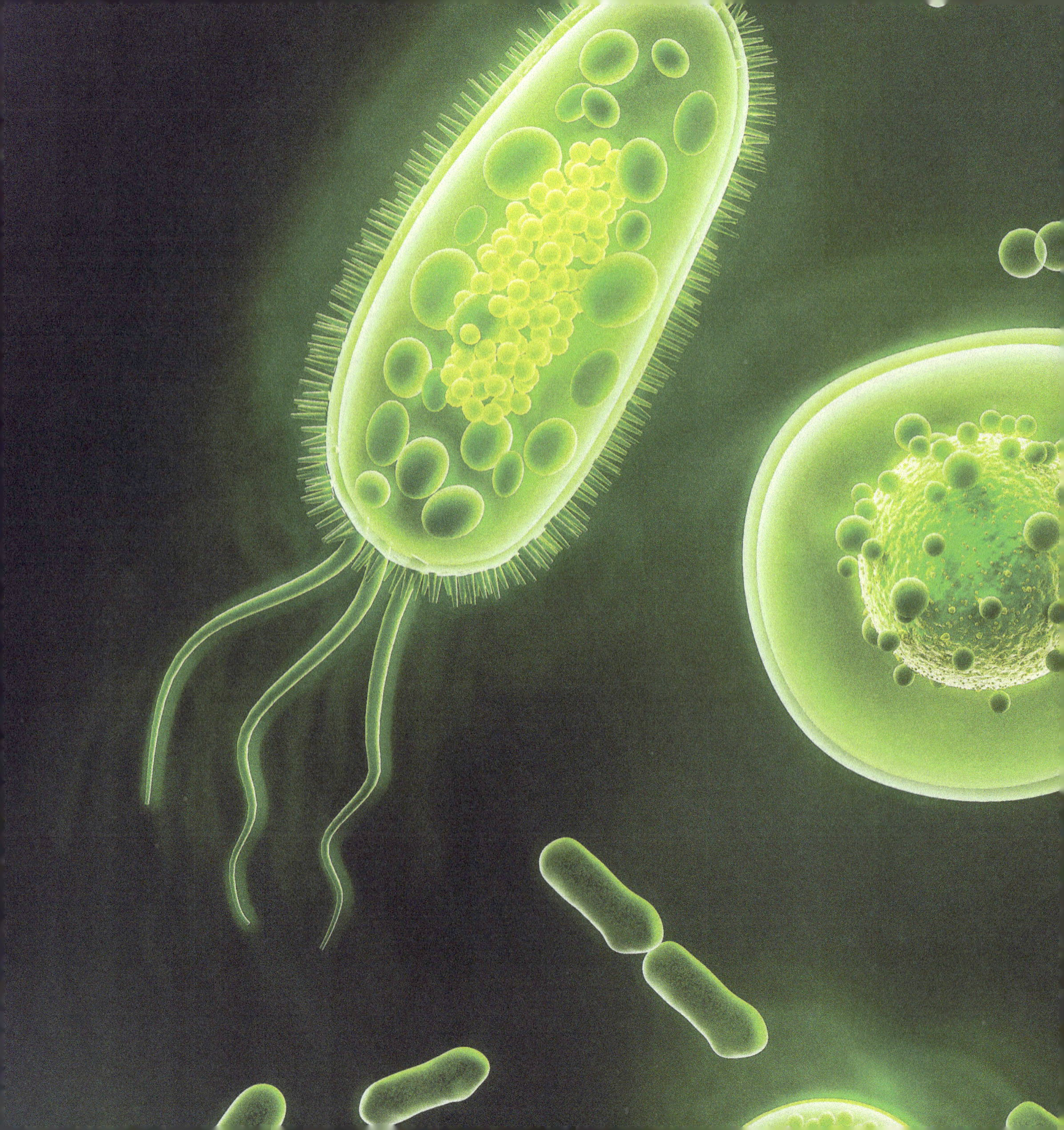

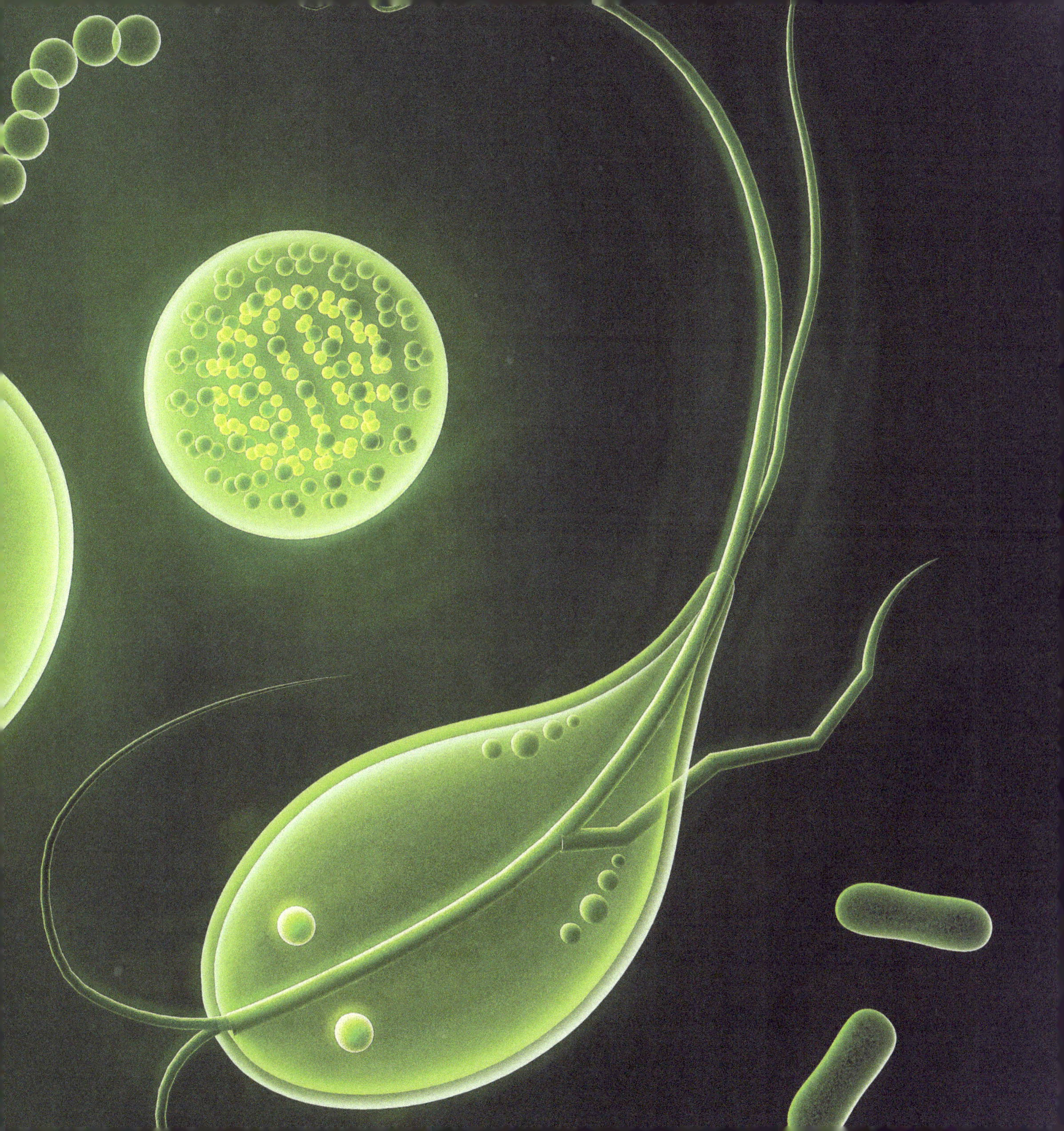

PSEUDOMONAS PUTIDA

Pseudomonas putidosis is a type of infection caused by bacteria. It is a potentially fatal bacterium that can lead to bacteremia.

The infection can also cause respiratory problems and can be passed from one person to another during medical procedures.

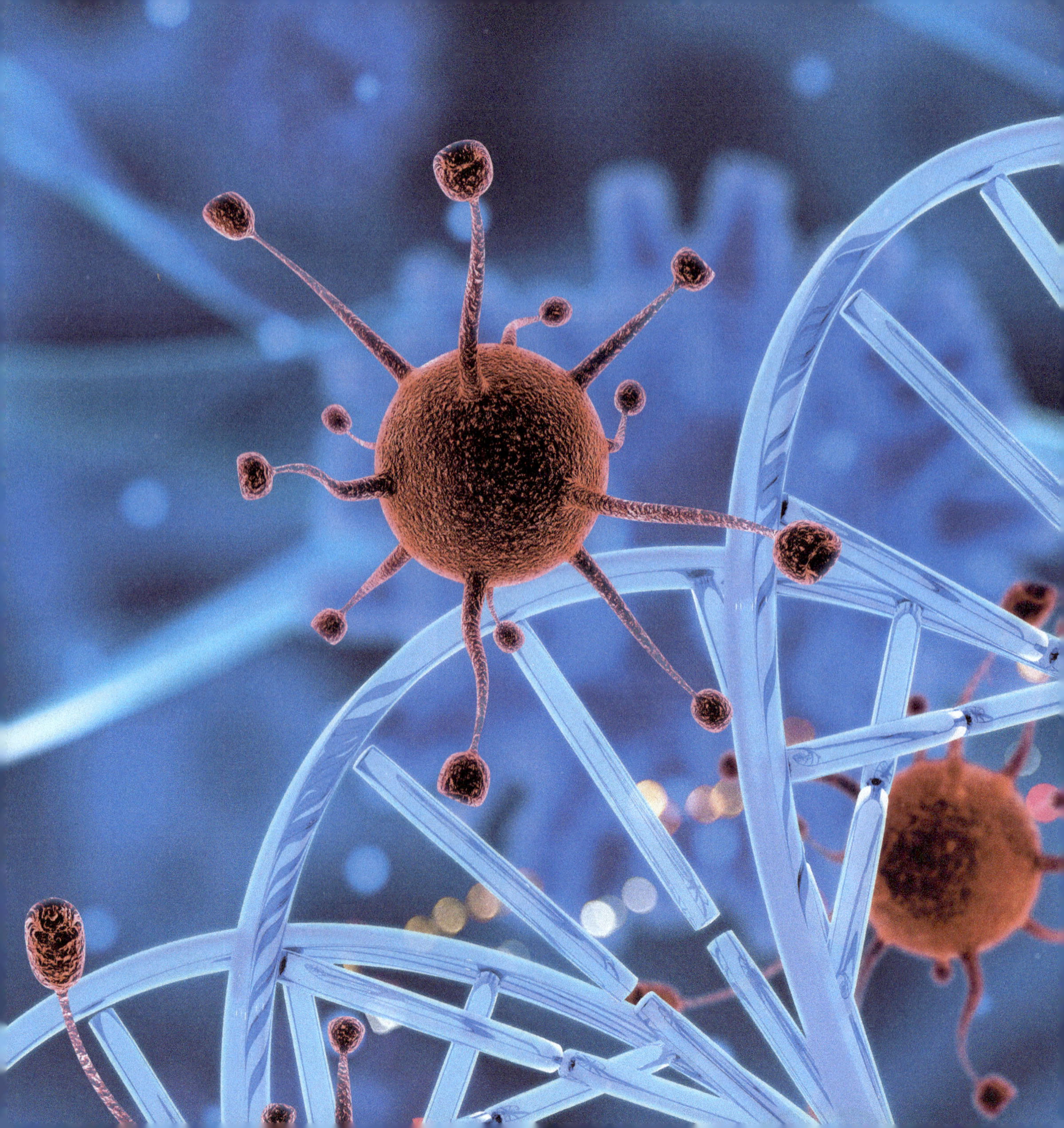

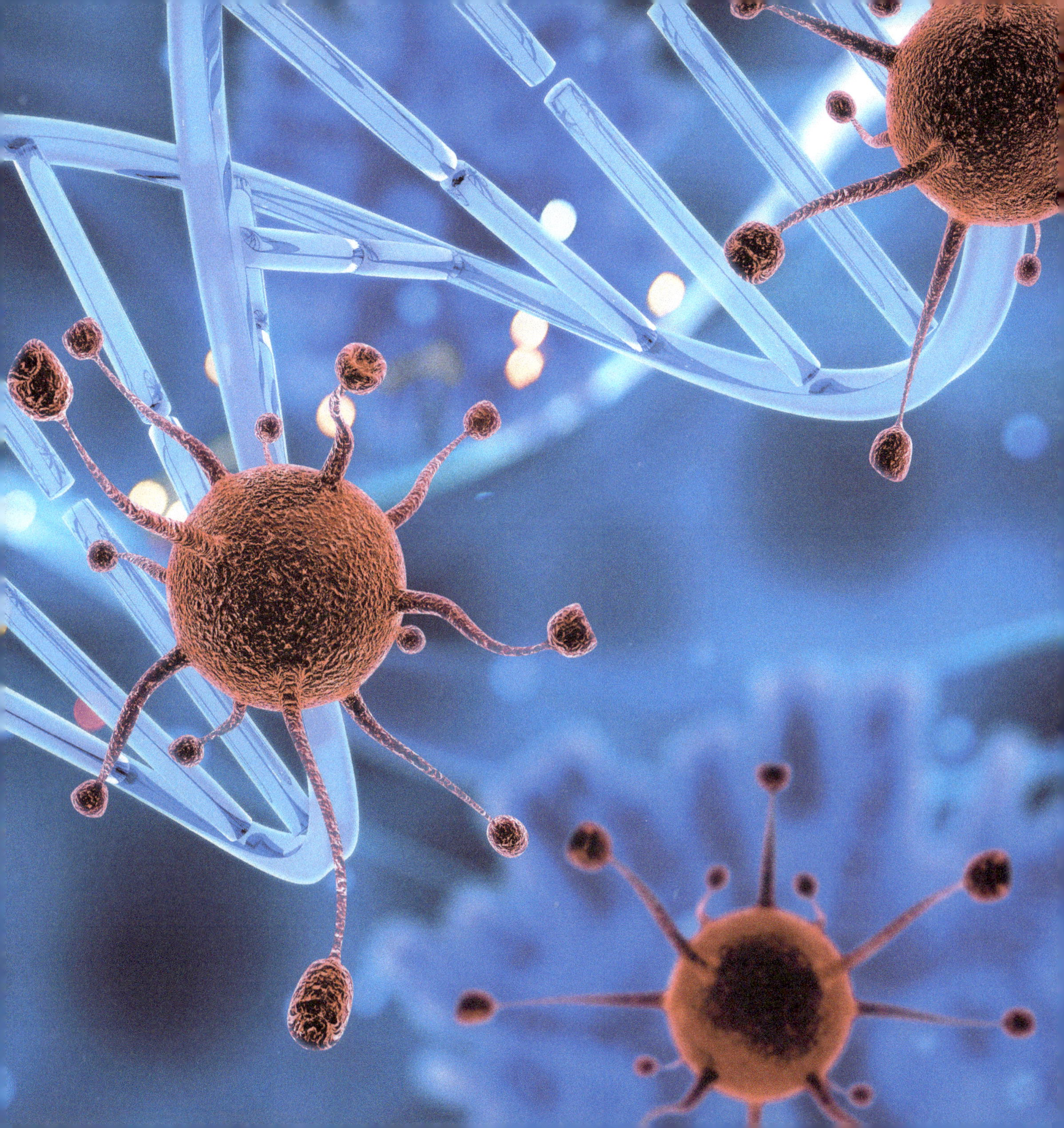

The microbe is usually isolated from clinical samples using biochemical tests. The organism can be differentiated from other Pseudomonas species using a gelatin hydrolysis test.

Other methods of identification include immunoassays, which are based on enzymes and proteins.

THIOMARGARITA NAMIBIENSIS

Thiomargarita namibiiensis is a microscopic bacterium that lives in sediments in the ocean. It is a lithotroph and feeds on sulfide and nitrate. The sulfides are a form of energy, and the nitrate is an electron acceptor.

Thioploca live in sediments that are rich in diatom shells, which increase the sulfide concentration. This enables the bacteria to survive in these layers and utilize the nutrients from a wide variety of substrates.

CPSIA information can be obtained
at www.ICGtesting.com
Printed in the USA
LVHW072040220323
742311LV00021B/1640

9 781071 718865